Gastric Sleeve Bariatric Cookbook for Beginners

Easy, Healthy & Delicious Recipes for Every Stage of Recovery Following

Bariatric Surgery

Sarch Scoter

Table of contents

Introduction

First, I want to congratulate you on the successful completion of your gastric sleeve bariatric surgery and thank you for choosing this book and it is my pleasure to help you on this journey.

Gastric sleeve is one of the surgical procedures makes your stomach smaller and help to lose your overweight. This procedure is known as sleeve gastronomy or it is known as vertical sleeve gastronomy. This procedure is one of the most popular types of bariatric surgery. In this procedure near about 75 to 80 percent, part of your stomach is removed permanently. After removing these parts your stomach is smaller than before. While removing a big part of your stomach gut hormones known as Ghrelin are removed in this procedure. These hormones are also called hunger hormones. The absence of these hormones helps you to control your appetite and you never feel hungry. After gastric sleeve bariatric surgery if you follow a proper diet plan you can reduce approximately 60 percent of overweight within 1-2 years' time. After the surgery, you have to make some adjustments with your food intake such as lower the intake of calories and carbohydrates, avoid sugary food, fibrous vegetables, starchy food. Increase the intake of protein-rich foods and drinks, liquid foods, etc.

The book contains simple and comprehensive information about gastric sleeve bariatric surgery and post-surgery diet plans along with healthy and delicious recipes allowed after gastric sleeve surgery. These recipes are divided into four different stages of diet after surgery. In this book, I have discovered many delicious recipes easy to make, tasty and Nutri rich shakes and smoothies along with some nutritious soft food combinations.

My goal here is that provides you all detailed information about gastric sleeve bariatric surgery and gastric sleeve diet. The book contains all information about the surgery and its benefits along with pre and post-surgery tips. There are various books available in the market on this subject. Thanks for choosing my book, I hope the book will help you to achieve your goal.

Chapter 1: Gastric Sleeve Surgery Basics

What is Gastric Sleeve Surgery

Gastric sleeve is one of the surgical procedures done for excess weight loss. During surgery, the procedure surgeon removes 75 to 80 percent of stomach curvature permanently with the help of laparoscopic surgery. After this surgery only the banana size vertical tube is left due to this it holds a small amount of food. Due to the reduction of stomach size, your stomach didn't accommodate more food. In a simple word, it helps to reduce your appetite and the need for food will be reduced. Such reduction of intake of food will automatically lead to weight loss. Gastric surgery is one of the popular choices for those people who have obesity and looking for extreme weight loss solutions. Scientific research and study show that gastric sleeve bariatric surgery is very effective for long term weight loss.

Most of the study over gastric sleeve surgery shows a reduction of 60 percent of total excess weight by adopting a strict diet and recommended exercise after surgery. After successful gastric surgery, you will start with liquid for a few weeks. You will allow in taking only pure instead of solid foods.

Benefits of Gastric Sleeve Surgery

There are various health benefits of gastric sleeve surgery. Here we have seen some of them are as follows:

1. Weight loss

Research and study show that after gastric sleeve surgery people lose near about 60 percent of excess body weight within 12 to 18 months. Eating the right food and exercising regularly helps you to maintain your weight after surgery. Gastric sleeve surgery provides you long term weight loss benefits.

2. Remission for Type 2 diabetes

The study conducted over type 2 diabetic patients shows that gastric sleeve surgery is very effective on type 2 diabetes. It helps to all diabetic patients to remain free from taking insulin and adjunct medications for 3 years after gastric surgery.

3. Helps to improve cardiovascular health

The gastric weight loss surgery helps to reduce the risk of peripheral heart disease, strokes, and coronary heart disease. It also helps to maintain your blood pressure and cholesterol level.

4. Relief from joint pain

Obesity and excess weight are puts lots of pressure on your weight-bearing joints. After gastric sleeve surgery due to significant weight loss gives relieves from stress from joint and gives joint pain relief.

5. Relief from depression

Due to obesity most people feel depressed because of social stigma and poor body image. They find difficulties to participate in social activities. After gastric surgery body losing their excess weight which helps to improve physical as well as emotional health in such peoples and given relief from depression.

Tips for Before Surgery

1. Change your diet plan

Change your regular diet and adopt a liquid-only diet two weeks before gastric sleeve bariatric surgery.

2. Quit Smoking

The peoples who smoke before their gastric surgery has higher chances to develop surgical site infection. Quit smoking at least one month before surgery helps you to recover fast after surgery. Smoking decreases your blood flow and increases complications after surgery.

3. Stock-up protein-rich food

Stock-up protein-rich soups, broth, sugar-free Popsicle, skim milk and protein-rich liquid meals. Afterward, you will need protein-rich food. You can also stock-up protein powder you like most along with low calories protein-rich food.

4. Prepare mentally before surgery

The patient should be aware of the implications of having gastric surgery. Also known detail information about the pros and cons after surgery. If you are not prepared mentally then make an appointment with a psychologist which will help you to become stronger mentally and emotionally.

5. Prepare your hospital checklist

Make your essential list and carry them with you in the hospital. Select comfortable and loose clothes, your regular medications, comfortable sleepers, books, magazines, and tablets or laptops during your overnight hospital stay.

6. Your support groups

Before gastric surgery makes sure that your immediate family and friends are aware of your needs after surgery.

7. Talk to your surgeon

Talk to your surgeon related to surgery. Tell him with all about your previous surgical and medical history.

Tips for After Surgery

1. Eat slower and measure your daily meal

This is one of the good habits to eat meals slowly and also measure the quantity of food intake. Eating too fast leads you towards overeating this will set you up for failure from your goal.

2. Consume enough protein

Consumption of enough protein daily after surgery will help you to heal faster, help to prevent loss of muscle mass and also help to maintain your body energy level. The carbohydrate meal is broken faster and reduces your hunger but instead of carbohydrates meal protein breaks down slowly and you will feel full. NuGo Slim is one of the best and essential protein supplements recommended most after gastric sleeve surgery.

3. Take your Vitamins and Supplements:

After gastric sleeve surgery, you need to reduce your meal down to 4 ounces. This means that you need to supplement vitamins because of low food consumption. You will face some difficulty to absorb vitamin B1, B6, and B12 so vitamin supplementation is necessary after gastric sleeve surgery.

4. Do some exercise

Regular exercise is one of the ways which helps you to maintain your body weight for the long term. It also helps to reduce the risk of chronic diseases like cancer, diabetes and heart disease. It also helps to improve your body flexibility.

5. Stay hydrated

To maintain your body function including body temperature, blood pressure, kidney functions and healthy skin you need to keep your body hydrated. Drinks plenty of water during the day will help you to keep hydrated and also control your hunger.

6. Change your habit for long term success

The long-term success of weight loss surgery totally depends upon change your habit. These habits increase physical activities, controlling daily food intake, focusing on intake of protein. Adopting new habits helps you to keep your weight off.

7. Do not drink your calories

Avoid high calories drinks and consume low calories drinks like sugar-free juice, water, and unsweetened ice tea. Some people nothing lose their weight after 4 months due to the intake of sugar.

Chapter 2: Gastric Sleeve Diet

What is a Gastric Sleeve Diet?

Gastric diet is one of the strict diet plans followed before and after gastric sleeve surgery. It strictly reduces the intake of calories and carbohydrates. These calories and carbohydrates are coming from sweets, pasta, and potatoes. During gastric sleeve diet, you have to consume liquid foods that are low in calories and high in protein. Protein helps to maintain your muscle mass and also helps to maintain your body energy level. Before two days of surgery, you have to switch to a clear liquid diet, such as sugar-free protein shake, decaffeinated coffee or tea, sugar-free popsicles, broth, and water. During gastric sleeve diet completely avoid caffeinated and carbonated beverages.

After gastric sleeve surgery, a person must follow a strict diet to recover your body and adjust with the smaller size of your stomach. The person with gastric sleeve surgery eats smaller and more frequent meals for the rest of their lives. The diet plan can be divided into four stages

1. Stage one diet: Clear Liquids

This stage is beginning in the first week after your gastric sleeve surgery. In this stage of the diet, only a few ounces of food drinks have been allowed. This will help your stomach heal without getting stretched by foods. The liquid diet includes:

- Water
- Thin soup and broth
- Skim milk
- Decaffeinated coffee and tea
- Sugar-free gelatin and popsicles
- Unsweetened juice

Avoid sugary liquids during the first week of gastric sleeve surgery. Consuming sugary drinks may lead to raising digestive problems and occurs negative side effect on surgery.

Also, avoid carbonated and caffeinated beverages. During the first week of surgery always stay your body hydrated just remember only drink a small amount of liquid at a time.

2. Stage two diet: Protein-rich Liquids

The stage two begins after five days of gastric sleeve surgery. During this stage, you have to allow consuming protein-rich shake and more liquids like Skimmed milk, unsweetened and blended fruit juice. During this stage, you experience to increase your appetite but you have to stick your diet plan for getting a positive result. The protein-rich liquid includes:

- Sugar-free protein shakes
- Thin creamed soup and broth
- Non-fat sugar-free puddings
- Low-carb yogurt
- Split pea or lentil soup
- All food in stage one

During stage two it recommends you to consume near about 3 liters of liquid diet per day. Avoid sugary and carbonated liquids during stage two.

3. Stage three diet: Puree

Stage three begins after two weeks of gastric sleeve surgery. It allows you to include pureed soft food into your diet. The foods like mashed potatoes, fat-free yogurts, thick and smooth soups, baked beans. You are allowed to eat these diets in small quantity about 4 to 5 times daily. Food allowed during stage three is:

- Puree no sugar added fruits.
- Tofu.
- Pureed peas and lentils.
- Eggs.
- Plain yogurt.
- Steamed or boiled vegetables.

4. Stage four diet: Solid Food

Stage four begins after the four weeks of gastric sleeve surgery. It allows you to take soft solid food in the diet. Try to consume protein-rich foods because it recommends that you should consume at least 60 grams of protein in your daily meal. At this stage, your stomach should be fit to handle solid food. During this stage, you can consume three meals with some snacks. The solid foods allowed in this stage are:

- Lentil and beans soup.
- Hot cereals.
- Fish
- Boil potatoes
- Soft fruits without skin
- Low-fat cheese
- Lean ground turkey, chicken, beef, pork.
- Cooked vegetables

During this stage, you should avoid the whole milk products, snacks, and sugary drinks, fibrous vegetables like broccoli, celery, asparagus, starchy foods like white potatoes, pasta and bread, spicy foods, processed and fried fast food, etc.

How does the Gastric Sleeve work?

After gastric sleeve surgery, your stomach is holding a smaller amount of food because during surgery near about 75 to 80 percent of parts of your stomach are removed from your body. It helps you to reduce your food carving and weight loss process.

The surgery also removes the part of the stomach that produces Ghrelin. Gherlin is one of the gut hormones produce into your stomach it is also called hunger hormones. Removing these hormones from your body will reduce your hunger feeling and also help to reduce your appetite. By removing these hormones from your stomach, you can easily reduce you're overweight.

Chapter 3: FAQs

- How much weight did I lose after surgery?

You will lose near about 60 percent of extra weight during the two years of time after gastric sleeve surgery. Most people achieve this in the first year after gastric sleeve surgery. This surgery gives you long term weight loss benefits.

- Can I smoke?

No, you can quit your smoking habit completely. It is good to quit smoking 6 to 7 weeks before the surgery. If you cannot quit smoking your body takes a longer time to heal after gastric sleeve surgery. It also decreases your blood flow and changes to increase the complication after surgery.

- What is stomach stapling?

When the surgeon performs surgery, they use a surgical staple gun during gastric sleeve surgery. It helps to stop the bleeding and tissues can also heal each other properly with the help of staples. A staple is closed in the shape of B.

- What happens with staples in the body?

Basically, staples are made up of titanium. If they are moved from their original position it won't cause any problem into your body. From another point of view, they are not magnetic so they are not set off by an X-ray machine at the airport while you are traveling somewhere.

- Which diet is best after surgery?

After surgery, your diet can be divided into four stages. In the first stage, the patient should allow in taking a clear liquid diet. The second stage includes protein-rich liquid for diet. The third stage includes puree for diet and finally, the fourth stage includes solid food for diet.

- What do I need to carry to the hospital?

This totally depends on your needs generally you can carry the things which make you comfortable. You must carry clean and loose cloths, lip balm, moisturizer, your grooming items, comfortable pillow, laptop or tablet, comfortable slippers, etc.

- Will's stomach removed part grows back after surgery?

No as mention in the surgery it is a permanent surgery. There is no chance to grow back removed the part and the surgery is not reversible at any condition.

- Which person is eligible for surgery?

Generally, the peoples who have a Body Mass Index (BMI) of 40 and higher, facing extreme obesity problems. Also, the people who have a BMI of 35 to 39.9 and facing extreme overweight conditions, type 2 diabetes and hypertension. All of these conditions are eligible for gastric sleeve bariatric surgery.

Chapter4: 8-Week Meal Plan

Day 1

Breakfast-Egg Salad

Lunch-Cucumber Tuna Salad

Dinner-Baked Dijon Salmon

Day 2

Breakfast-Scrambled Eggs

Lunch-Roasted Parmesan Cauliflower

Dinner-Dijon Chicken Thighs

Day 3

Breakfast-Veggie Egg Scramble

Lunch-Delicious Chicken Salad

Dinner-Herb Pork Chops

Day 4

Breakfast-Almond Peanut Butter Oatmeal

Lunch-Cauliflower Mushroom Soup

Dinner-Taco Chicken

Day 5

Breakfast-Breakfast Kale Muffins

Lunch-Creamy Cauliflower Soup

Dinner-Broiled Fish Fillet

Day 6

Breakfast-Chocolate Overnight Oats

Lunch-Cauliflower Mash

Dinner-Yummy Chicken Bites

Day 7

Breakfast-Pumpkin Muffins

Lunch-Curried Egg Salad

Dinner-Grilled Chicken Breasts

Day 8

Breakfast-Almond Oatmeal

Lunch-Dijon Potato Salad

Dinner-Chili Garlic Salmon

Day 9

Breakfast-Vegetable Breakfast Quiche

Lunch-Carrot Sweet Potato Soup

Dinner-Baked Lemon Tilapia

Day 10

Breakfast-Mushroom Frittata

Lunch-Creamy Salmon Salad

Dinner-Garlic Shrimp

Day 11

Breakfast-Smooth Squash Mash

Lunch-Creamy Tomato Soup

Dinner-Garlic Shrimp

Day 12

Breakfast-Creamy Carrot Mash

Lunch-Healthy Spinach Soup

Dinner-Baked Lemon Tilapia

Day 13

Breakfast-Almond Raspberry Smoothie

Lunch-Healthy Spinach Soup

Dinner-Chili Garlic Salmon

Day 14

Breakfast-Coconut Strawberry Protein Smoothie

Lunch-Creamy Tomato Soup

Dinner-Grilled Chicken Breasts

Day 15

Breakfast-Coconut Strawberry Protein Smoothie

Lunch-Creamy Salmon Salad

Dinner-Yummy Chicken Bites

Day 16

Breakfast-Almond Raspberry Smoothie

Lunch-Carrot Sweet Potato Soup

Dinner-Broiled Fish Fillet

Day 17

Breakfast-Healthy Carrot Mash

Lunch-Dijon Potato Salad

Dinner-Taco Chicken

Day 18

Breakfast-Creamy Carrot Mash

Lunch-Curried Egg Salad

Dinner-Herb Pork Chops

Day 19

Breakfast-Smooth Squash Mash

Lunch-Cauliflower Mash

Dinner-Dijon Chicken Thighs

Day 20

Breakfast-Mushroom Frittata

Lunch-Creamy Cauliflower Soup

Dinner-Baked Dijon Salmon

Day 21

Breakfast-Vegetable Breakfast Quiche

Lunch-Cauliflower Mushroom Soup

Dinner-Yummy Chicken Bites

Day 22

Breakfast-Almond Oatmeal

Lunch-Delicious Chicken Salad

Dinner-Grilled Chicken Breasts

Day 23

Breakfast-Pumpkin Muffins

Lunch-Roasted Parmesan Cauliflower

Dinner-Chili Garlic Salmon

Day 24

Breakfast-Chocolate Overnight Oats

Lunch-Cucumber Tuna Salad

Dinner-Baked Lemon Tilapia

Day 25

Breakfast-Breakfast Kale Muffins

Lunch-Curried Egg Salad

Dinner-Garlic Shrimp

Day 26

Breakfast-Almond Peanut Butter Oatmeal

Lunch-Dijon Potato Salad

Dinner-Baked Dijon Salmon

Day 27

Breakfast-Veggie Egg Scramble

Lunch-Carrot Sweet Potato Soup

Dinner-Dijon Chicken Thighs

Day 28

Breakfast-Scrambled Eggs

Lunch-Creamy Salmon Salad

Dinner-Herb Pork Chops

Day 29

Breakfast-Egg Salad

Lunch-Creamy Tomato Soup

Dinner-Taco Chicken

Day 30

Breakfast-Coconut Strawberry Protein Smoothie

Lunch-Healthy Spinach Soup

Dinner-Broiled Fish Fillet

Day 31

Breakfast-Almond Raspberry Smoothie

Lunch-Cucumber Tuna Salad

Dinner-Garlic Shrimp

Day 32

Breakfast-Healthy Carrot Mash

Lunch-Roasted Parmesan Cauliflower

Dinner-Baked Lemon Tilapia

Day 33

Breakfast-Creamy Carrot Mash

Lunch-Delicious Chicken Salad

Dinner-Chili Garlic Salmon

Day 34

Breakfast-Smooth Squash Mash

Lunch-Cauliflower Mushroom Soup

Dinner-Grilled Chicken Breasts

Day 35

Breakfast-Mushroom Frittata

Lunch-Creamy Cauliflower Soup

Dinner-Yummy Chicken Bites

Day 36

Breakfast-Vegetable Breakfast Quiche

Lunch-Cauliflower Mash

Dinner-Broiled Fish Fillet

Day 37

Breakfast-Almond Oatmeal

Lunch-Healthy Spinach Soup

Dinner-Taco Chicken

Day 38

Breakfast-Pumpkin Muffins

Lunch-Creamy Tomato Soup

Dinner-Herb Pork Chops

Day 39

Breakfast-Chocolate Overnight Oats

Lunch-Creamy Salmon Salad

Dinner-Dijon Chicken Thighs

Day 40

Breakfast-Breakfast Kale Muffins

Lunch-Carrot Sweet Potato Soup

Dinner-Baked Dijon Salmon

Day 41

Breakfast-Almond Peanut Butter Oatmeal

Lunch-Dijon Potato Salad

Dinner-Yummy Chicken Bites

Day 42

Breakfast-Veggie Egg Scramble

Lunch-Curried Egg Salad

Dinner-Grilled Chicken Breasts

Day 43

Breakfast-Scrambled Eggs

Lunch-Cauliflower Mash

Dinner-Chili Garlic Salmon

Day 44

Breakfast-Egg Salad

Lunch-Creamy Cauliflower Soup

Dinner-Baked Lemon Tilapia

Day 45

Breakfast-Egg Salad

Lunch-Cauliflower Mushroom Soup

Dinner-Garlic Shrimp

Day 46

Breakfast-Scrambled Eggs

Lunch-Delicious Chicken Salad

Dinner-Baked Dijon Salmon

Day 47

Breakfast-Veggie Egg Scramble

Lunch-Roasted Parmesan Cauliflower

Dinner-Dijon Chicken Thighs

Day 48

Breakfast-Almond Peanut Butter Oatmeal

Lunch-Cucumber Tuna Salad

Dinner-Herb Pork Chops

Day 49

Breakfast-Breakfast Kale Muffins

Lunch-Cucumber Tuna Salad

Dinner-Taco Chicken

Day 50

Breakfast-Chocolate Overnight Oats

Lunch-Roasted Parmesan Cauliflower

Dinner-Broiled Fish Fillet

Day 51

Breakfast-Pumpkin Muffins

Lunch-Delicious Chicken Salad

Dinner-Taco Chicken

Day 52

Breakfast-Almond Oatmeal

Lunch-Cauliflower Mushroom Soup

Dinner-Broiled Fish Fillet

Day 53

Breakfast-Vegetable Breakfast Quiche

Lunch-Creamy Cauliflower Soup

Dinner-Yummy Chicken Bites

Day 54

Breakfast-Mushroom Frittata

Lunch-Cauliflower Mash

Dinner-Grilled Chicken Breasts

Day 55

Breakfast-Smooth Squash Mash

Lunch-Curried Egg Salad

Dinner-Chili Garlic Salmon

Day 56

Breakfast- Almond Oatmeal

Lunch-Dijon Potato Salad

Dinner-Baked Lemon Tilapia

Chapter5: 4 Stages after Surgery

Stage1: Clear Fluids

Cinnamon Lemon Tea

Preparation Time: 5 minutes

Cooking Time: 5 minutes

Serve: 1

Ingredients:

- 1/2 lemon, cut into wedges
- 1 cup of water
- 1 tsp cinnamon

Directions:

1. Add water in a small saucepan and bring to boil.
2. Add cinnamon and stir until cinnamon is dissolved.
3. Squeeze lemon into the tea. Stir well.
4. Serve hot and enjoy.

Nutritional Value (Amount per Serving):

- Calories 9
- Fat 0.1 g
- Carbohydrates 2.5 g
- Sugar 0.3 g
- Protein 0.2 g
- Cholesterol 0 mg

Turmeric Tea

Preparation Time: 5 minutes

Cooking Time: 5 minutes

Serve: 2

Ingredients:

- 1/4 tsp ginger powder
- 1/4 tsp turmeric
- 2 cups of water
- 1 tbsp raw honey
- Pinch of black pepper

Directions:

1. Add water in a small saucepan and bring to boil.
2. Remove saucepan from heat.
3. Add ginger powder and turmeric. Stir and set aside for 5 minutes.
4. Strain hot tea and pour it into cups.
5. Stir in honey and black pepper.
6. Serve hot and enjoy.

Nutritional Value (Amount per Serving):

- Calories 35
- Fat 0 g
- Carbohydrates 8 g
- Sugar 7 g
- Protein 0.1 g
- Cholesterol 0 mg

Basil Tea

Preparation Time: 5 minutes

Cooking Time: 10 minutes

Serve: 1

Ingredients:

- 1 tbsp basil, dried
- 1 cup of water
- 1 tsp honey

Directions:

1. Add basil in boiling water and set aside for 10 minutes.
2. Strain and add honey.
3. Stir well and serve hot.

Nutritional Value (Amount per Serving):

- Calories 20
- Fat 0 g
- Carbohydrates 4 g
- Sugar 4 g
- Protein 0.1 g
- Cholesterol 0 mg

Strawberry Cucumber Thyme Infused Water

Preparation Time: 5 minutes

Cooking Time: 5 minutes

Serve: 4

Ingredients:

- 1/2 cup fresh strawberries, sliced
- 4 cups of water
- 1 cucumber, sliced
- 5 sprig thyme

Directions:

1. Add thyme, cucumber, and strawberries in a glass jar.
2. Pour water into the jar and stir well.
3. Place jar in the refrigerator for 1 hour.
4. Serve and enjoy.

Nutritional Value (Amount per Serving):

- Calories 21
- Fat 0.2 g
- Carbohydrates 4 g
- Sugar 2 g
- Protein 10 g
- Cholesterol 0 mg

Mint Orange Infused Water

Preparation Time: 5 minutes

Cooking Time: 5 minutes

Serve: 4

Ingredients:

- 10 fresh mint leaves
- 4 cups of water
- 1 apple, sliced
- 1/2 cup grapes
- 1 orange, sliced

Directions:

1. Add grapes sliced orange, apple and mint leaves in a glass jar.
2. Pour water into the jar and stir well.
3. Place jar in the refrigerator for 1 hour.
4. Serve and enjoy.

Nutritional Value (Amount per Serving):

- Calories 66
- Fat 0.3 g
- Carbohydrates 15 g
- Sugar 8 g
- Protein 1.2 g
- Cholesterol 0 mg

Watermelon Mint Infused Water

Preparation Time: 5 minutes

Cooking Time: 5 minutes

Serve: 4

Ingredients:

- 1 1/2 cups watermelon, sliced
- 4 cups of water
- 8 fresh mint leaves

Directions:

1. Add mint and watermelon in a glass jar.
2. Pour water into the jar and cover jar with a lid.
3. Place jar in the refrigerator for 1 hour.
4. Serve and enjoy.

Nutritional Value (Amount per Serving):

- Calories 25
- Fat 0.3 g
- Carbohydrates 6 g
- Sugar 3 g
- Protein 1.2 g
- Cholesterol 0 mg

Strawberry Mint Infused Water

Preparation Time: 5 minutes

Cooking Time: 5 minutes

Serve: 2

Ingredients:

- 4 strawberries, sliced
- 1 cucumber, sliced
- 5 fresh mint leaves
- 2 cups of water

Directions:

1. Add cucumber, strawberries, and mint in a glass jar.
2. Pour water into the jar and stir well.
3. Cover jar with lid and place in the refrigerator for 1 hour.
4. Serve and enjoy.

Nutritional Value (Amount per Serving):

- Calories 40
- Fat 0.4 g
- Carbohydrates 8 g
- Sugar 3.7 g
- Protein 2 g
- Cholesterol 0 mg

Lemon Melon Popsicle

Preparation Time: 5 minutes

Cooking Time: 4 minutes

Serve: 4

Ingredients:

- 3 cups melon, chopped
- 3 drops liquid stevia
- 1 tsp fresh lemon juice

Directions:

1. Add all ingredients into the blender and blend until smooth.
2. Pour melon mixture into the Popsicle molds.
3. Place in the refrigerator for 4 hours or until set.
4. Serve and enjoy.

Nutritional Value (Amount per Serving):

- Calories 41
- Fat 0.2 g
- Carbohydrates 8 g
- Sugar 8 g
- Protein 1 g
- Cholesterol 0 mg

Raspberry Popsicle

Preparation Time: 5 minutes

Cooking Time: 5 minutes

Serve: 6

Ingredients:

- 4 cups frozen raspberries
- 6 drops liquid stevia
- 1 1/2 cups fresh grapefruit juice

Directions:

1. Add all ingredients into the blender and blend until smooth.
2. Pour raspberry mixture into the Popsicle molds and place in the refrigerator for 3-4 hours.
3. Serve and enjoy.

Nutritional Value (Amount per Serving):

- Calories 61
- Fat 0.6 g
- Carbohydrates 14 g
- Sugar 7 g
- Protein 1.3 g
- Cholesterol 0 mg

Refreshing Strawberry Limeade

Preparation Time: 5 minutes
Cooking Time: 5 minutes
Serve: 1

Ingredients:

- 1/4 tsp strawberry extract
- 1/2 fresh lime juice
- 1 1/2 cup cold water
- 1/2 cup ice

Directions:

1. Add all ingredients into the serving glass and stir well.
2. Serve and enjoy.

Nutritional Value (Amount per Serving):

- Calories 8
- Fat 0 g
- Carbohydrates 2 g
- Sugar 0.4 g
- Protein 0.1 g
- Cholesterol 0 mg

Stage2: Full Liquids

Chocolate Peanut Butter Shake

Preparation Time: 5 minutes

Cooking Time: 5 minutes

Serve: 1

Ingredients:

- 1 scoop vanilla protein powder
- 1 tbsp unsweetened cocoa powder
- 1 tbsp chia seeds
- 2 tbsp rolled oats
- 2 tbsp powdered peanut butter
- ½ cup unsweetened almond milk
- ½ banana
- ¼ cup ice

Directions:

1. Add all ingredients into the blender and blend until smooth and creamy.
2. Serve and enjoy.

Nutritional Value (Amount per Serving):

- Calories 316
- Fat 7.1 g
- Carbohydrates 29 g
- Sugar 8.4 g
- Protein 37.4 g
- Cholesterol 2 mg

Peach Blueberry Protein Shake

Preparation Time: 5 minutes

Cooking Time: 5 minutes

Serve: 2

Ingredients:

- ½ cup frozen peach slices
- ½ cup frozen blueberries
- 1 tbsp chia seeds
- 8 oz unsweetened coconut milk
- ½ avocado, diced
- 1 scoop vanilla protein powder

Directions:

1. Add all ingredients into the blender and blend until smooth and creamy.
2. Serve and enjoy.

Nutritional Value (Amount per Serving):

- Calories 234
- Fat 13 g
- Carbohydrates 15.9 g
- Sugar 7.7 g
- Protein 15.9 g
- Cholesterol 1 mg

Chocolate Milkshake

Preparation Time: 5 minutes

Cooking Time: 5 minutes

Serve: 1

Ingredients:

- 1 tbsp unsweetened cocoa powder
- 1/2 avocado
- 1/2 cup ice
- 1 tbsp swerve
- 1/2 tsp vanilla
- 1/2 cup coconut milk
- Pinch of Himalayan salt

Directions:

1. Add all ingredients into the blender and blend until smooth and creamy.
2. Serve and enjoy.

Nutritional Value (Amount per Serving):

- Calories 116
- Fat 9 g
- Carbohydrates 8.1 g
- Sugar 0.5 g
- Protein 2 g
- Cholesterol 0 mg

Apple Peanut Butter Shake

Preparation Time: 5 minutes

Cooking Time: 5 minutes

Serve: 1

Ingredients:

- 1/2 apple, peel and diced
- 2 tbsp peanut powder
- 3/4 cup ice
- 1 scoop chocolate protein powder
- 8 oz unsweetened almond milk

Directions:

1. Add all ingredients into the blender and blend until smooth and creamy.
2. Serve and enjoy.

Nutritional Value (Amount per Serving):

- Calories 203
- Fat 1.5 g
- Carbohydrates 14 g
- Sugar 8 g
- Protein 32.5 g
- Cholesterol 4 mg

Almond Protein Shake

Preparation Time: 5 minutes
Cooking Time: 5 minutes
Serve: 1

Ingredients:

- 2 tbsp almonds
- 1 scoop chocolate protein powder
- 12 oz unsweetened almond milk
- 1 cup ice
- 2 tbsp coconut flakes

Directions:

1. Add all ingredients into the blender and blend until smooth and creamy.
2. Serve and enjoy.

Nutritional Value (Amount per Serving):

- Calories 214
- Fat 14 g
- Carbohydrates 8.8 g
- Sugar 2.1 g
- Protein 14 g
- Cholesterol 20 mg

Almond Butter Shake

Preparation Time: 5 minutes

Cooking Time: 5 minutes

Serve: 1

Ingredients:

- 3 tbsp almond butter
- 1 cup unsweetened almond milk
- 1/2 cup ice
- 6 drops liquid stevia
- 1 tbsp coconut oil
- 1 tbsp unsweetened cocoa powder

Directions:

1. Add all ingredients into the blender and blend until smooth and creamy.
2. Serve and enjoy.

Nutritional Value (Amount per Serving):

- Calories 245
- Fat 25 g
- Carbohydrates 8.5 g
- Sugar 1 g
- Protein 6 g
- Cholesterol 0 mg

Chocó Blackberry Shake

Preparation Time: 5 minutes

Cooking Time: 5 minutes

Serve: 1

Ingredients:

- 1/4 cup blackberries
- 1 cup unsweetened coconut milk
- 1/2 cup ice
- 2 tbsp MCT oil
- 1/4 tsp xanthan gum
- 8 drops liquid stevia
- 2 tbsp unsweetened cocoa powder

Directions:

1. Add all ingredients into the blender and blend until smooth and creamy.
2. Serve and enjoy.

Nutritional Value (Amount per Serving):

- Calories 285
- Fat 33 g
- Carbohydrates 12 g
- Sugar 2 g
- Protein 2.5 g
- Cholesterol 0 mg

Vanilla Strawberry Milkshake

Preparation Time: 5 minutes

Cooking Time: 5 minutes

Serve: 1

Ingredients:

- 1/2 cup fresh strawberries
- 1 cup unsweetened almond milk
- 1/2 tsp vanilla
- 1 tbsp coconut oil
- 1/4 cup coconut milk
- 6 drops liquid stevia

Directions:

1. Add all ingredients into the blender and blend until smooth and creamy.
2. Serve and enjoy.

Nutritional Value (Amount per Serving):

- Calories 315
- Fat 31 g
- Carbohydrates 10.6 g
- Sugar 5 g
- Protein 2.6 g
- Cholesterol 0 mg

Almond Raspberry Smoothie

Preparation Time: 5 minutes

Cooking Time: 5 minutes

Serve: 2

Ingredients:

- 1 1/2 cups frozen raspberries
- 1 1/2 cups unsweetened almond milk
- 3/4 cup low-fat yogurt

Directions:

1. Add all ingredients into the blender and blend until smooth and creamy.
2. Serve and enjoy.

Nutritional Value (Amount per Serving):

- Calories 130
- Fat 6 g
- Carbohydrates 14 g
- Sugar 8 g
- Protein 5 g
- Cholesterol 15 mg

Coconut Strawberry Protein Smoothie

Preparation Time: 5 minutes
Cooking Time: 5 minutes
Serve: 2

Ingredients:

- 2 cups frozen strawberries
- 1 tsp vanilla
- 1 scoop protein powder
- 1 can coconut milk

Directions:

1. Add all ingredients into the blender and blend until smooth and creamy.
2. Serve and enjoy.

Nutritional Value (Amount per Serving):

- Calories 146
- Fat 7 g
- Carbohydrates 11 g
- Sugar 4 g
- Protein 10 g
- Cholesterol 30 mg

Stage3: Soft Foods Recipes

Delicious Pureed Chicken

Preparation Time: 10 minutes

Cooking Time: 5 minutes

Serve: 2

Ingredients:

- 1 chicken breast, skinless, boneless, and cooked
- 1/8 tsp onion powder
- 2 tbsp light mayonnaise
- 2 tbsp low-fat yogurt
- Pepper
- Salt

Directions:

1. Add chicken breast into the food processor and process until getting a fine consistency.
2. Add remaining ingredients and stir everything well.
3. Serve and enjoy.

Nutritional Value (Amount per Serving):

- Calories 133
- Fat 6.5 g
- Carbohydrates 4.7 g
- Sugar 2.1 g
- Protein 12.9 g
- Cholesterol 41 mg

Pureed Pinto Beans

Preparation Time: 10 minutes
Cooking Time: 10 minutes
Serve: 4

Ingredients:

- 14.5 oz can pinto beans
- 1 scoop protein powder
- 2 tbsp vegetable stock
- 1 ½ tbsp salsa

Directions:

1. Add all ingredients into the saucepan and heat over medium heat until just warm. Stir well.
2. Transfer beans mixture to the blender and blends until smooth.
3. Serve and enjoy.

Nutritional Value (Amount per Serving):

- Calories 127
- Fat 0.5 g
- Carbohydrates 19.5 g
- Sugar 2 g
- Protein 12 g
- Cholesterol 16 mg

Pureed Tuna

Preparation Time: 5 minutes

Cooking Time: 5 minutes

Serve: 4

Ingredients:

- 6 oz can tuna
- 2 tbsp low-fat yogurt
- 1 tbsp low-fat mayonnaise
- Pepper
- Salt

Directions:

1. Add tuna in the food processor and process until tuna is shredded.
2. Add remaining ingredients and stir everything well.
3. Serve and enjoy.

Nutritional Value (Amount per Serving):

- Calories 69
- Fat 1.7 g
- Carbohydrates 1.4 g
- Sugar 0.8 g
- Protein 11.3 g
- Cholesterol 14 mg

Healthy Salmon Pate

Preparation Time: 5 minutes
Cooking Time: 5 minutes
Serve: 1

Ingredients:

- 2.5 oz smoked salmon
- 1 tbsp fresh lemon juice
- ¼ tsp dried dill
- 2 tbsp low-fat yogurt
- Pepper
- Salt

Directions:

1. Add all ingredients except yogurt into the food processor and process until salmon is nicely diced.
2. Add yogurt and stir everything well.
3. Serve and enjoy.

Nutritional Value (Amount per Serving):

- Calories 109
- Fat 3.6 g
- Carbohydrates 2.7 g
- Sugar 2.5 g
- Protein 14.9 g
- Cholesterol 18 mg

Smooth Squash Mash

Preparation Time: 10 minutes

Cooking Time: 30 minutes

Serve: 8

Ingredients:

- 3 lbs butternut squash, chopped
- 1/2 tsp cinnamon
- 1/4 cup unsweetened coconut milk
- 1/2 tsp oregano
- 1/2 tsp garlic, minced
- 2 tbsp olive oil

Directions:

1. Preheat the oven to 350 F/ 180 C.
2. In a bowl, add butternut squash, oregano, olive oil, and garlic and toss well.
3. Transfer squash on a baking tray and bake for 30 minutes.
4. Combine together coconut milk and cinnamon and set aside.
5. Remove baked squash from the oven and let it cool for 5 minutes.
6. Add squash in a blender and blend until smooth.
7. Add almond milk mixture and blend until well combined.
8. Serve and enjoy.

Nutritional Value (Amount per Serving):

- Calories 126
- Fat 5 g
- Carbohydrates 20 g
- Sugar 4 g
- Protein 2 g
- Cholesterol 0 mg

Creamy Carrot Mash

Preparation Time: 10 minutes

Cooking Time: 15 minutes

Serve: 4

Ingredients:

- 6 medium carrots, peeled and diced
- 2 large potatoes, peeled and diced
- 2 tbsp butter
- 1/2 tsp coriander powder
- 1/2 tsp paprika
- 3 tbsp heavy cream
- Pepper
- Salt

Directions:

1. Add carrot and potato in a large pot and cover with water.
2. Bring to boil for 15 minutes or until tender. Drain well.
3. Add cream, butter, paprika, and coriander powder and stir well.
4. Mash carrot and potato until smooth.
5. Season with pepper and salt.
6. Serve and enjoy.

Nutritional Value (Amount per Serving):

- Calories 271
- Fat 10 g
- Carbohydrates 35 g
- Sugar 6 g
- Protein 4 g
- Cholesterol 36 mg

Healthy Carrot Mash

Preparation Time: 10 minutes

Cooking Time: 15 minutes

Serve: 4

Ingredients:

- 2 lbs carrots, peeled and chopped
- 1/2 cup vegetable broth
- 1 tsp garlic powder
- 1/4 tsp onion powder
- 4 tbsp butter
- Pepper
- Salt

Directions:

1. Add water in a large pot and bring to boil.
2. Add carrot in a pot and cook for 15 minutes or until tender.
3. Drain well and return carrot to the pot.
4. Add broth, butter, pepper, garlic powder, onion powder, and salt.
5. Mash carrots using masher until smooth.
6. Serve and enjoy.

Nutritional Value (Amount per Serving):

- Calories 201
- Fat 10 g
- Carbohydrates 23 g
- Sugar 10 g
- Protein 2 g
- Cholesterol 30 mg

Broccoli Cauliflower Mash

Preparation Time: 10 minutes
Cooking Time: 15 minutes
Serve: 4

Ingredients:

- 4 cups broccoli florets
- 4 cups cauliflower florets
- 1/4 tsp onion powder
- 1/4 tsp garlic powder
- 2 tbsp butter, melted
- 2 cups vegetable stock
- 2 tbsp fresh parsley
- 1 tsp sea salt

Directions:

1. Add broccoli florets and cauliflower florets in steamer and steam for 15 minutes.
2. Transfer cauliflower and broccoli in a blender along with butter, stock, garlic powder, onion powder, and parsley and blend until smooth.
3. Season with salt and serve.

Nutritional Value (Amount per Serving):

- Calories 111
- Fat 6.7 g
- Carbohydrates 12.2 g
- Sugar 4.6 g
- Protein 4.7 g
- Cholesterol 15 mg

Creamy Tomato Soup

Preparation Time: 10 minutes
Cooking Time: 40 minutes
Serve: 4

Ingredients:

- 1 lb fresh tomatoes, halved
- 15 oz can tomatoes
- 2 red bell peppers, sliced
- 1 tbsp olive oil
- 2 cups vegetable stock
- Pepper
- Salt

Directions:

1. Preheat the oven to 400 F/ 200 C.
2. Place tomatoes and bell peppers on a baking tray and drizzle with oil.
3. Roast in preheated oven for 20 minutes.
4. Transfer roasted tomatoes and peppers to the saucepan along with remaining ingredients and cook over medium heat for 15-20 minutes.
5. Puree the soup using blender until smooth and creamy.
6. Season with pepper and salt.
7. Serve and enjoy.

Nutritional Value (Amount per Serving):

- Calories 97
- Fat 4.9 g
- Carbohydrates 15.4 g
- Sugar 10.6 g
- Protein 2.6 g
- Cholesterol 0 mg

Healthy Spinach Soup

Preparation Time: 10 minutes

Cooking Time: 15 minutes

Serve: 4

Ingredients:

- 10.5 oz spinach, wash and chopped
- 2 potatoes, peeled and diced
- 2 1/2 cups vegetable stock
- 1/4 tsp garlic powder
- 1 tbsp olive oil
- Pepper
- Salt

Directions:

1. Heat oil in a saucepan over medium heat.
2. Add spinach and cook until wilted.
3. Add potatoes, garlic powder, and stock and cook for 15-20 minutes.
4. Puree the soup using blender until smooth.
5. Season with pepper and salt.
6. Serve and enjoy.

Nutritional Value (Amount per Serving):

- Calories 124
- Fat 4.4 g
- Carbohydrates 20.1 g
- Sugar 2.1 g
- Protein 4 g
- Cholesterol 0 mg

Stage4: Solid Foods

Breakfast

Egg Salad

Preparation Time: 10 minutes
Cooking Time: 5 minutes
Serve: 2

Ingredients:

- 5 hard-boiled eggs, peeled and chopped
- 1/8 tsp mustard
- ½ tsp onion powder
- 1/3 cup low-fat cottage cheese
- ¼ tsp salt

Directions:

1. Add all ingredients into the mixing bowl and mix well.
2. Serve and enjoy.

Nutritional Value (Amount per Serving):

- Calories 194
- Fat 11.7 g
- Carbohydrates 2.8 g
- Sugar 1.2 g
- Protein 19.1 g
- Cholesterol 412 mg

Scrambled Eggs

Preparation Time: 10 minutes
Cooking Time: 5 minutes
Serve: 1

Ingredients:

- 3 eggs, lightly beaten
- 2 tbsp chives, chopped
- ½ cup ricotta
- 1 tbsp butter
- Pepper
- Salt

Directions:

1. Melt butter in a pan over medium heat.
2. In a bowl, whisk together eggs, chives, ricotta, pepper, and salt and pour into the pan.
3. Gently stir egg mixture until eggs are cooked and scrambled, about 5 minutes.
4. Serve and enjoy.

Nutritional Value (Amount per Serving):

- Calories 464
- Fat 34.5 g
- Carbohydrates 7.7 g
- Sugar 1.5 g
- Protein 31.1 g
- Cholesterol 560 mg

Veggie Egg Scramble

Preparation Time: 10 minutes
Cooking Time: 10 minutes
Serve: 1

Ingredients:

- 3 eggs, lightly beaten
- 1/4 cup bell peppers, chopped
- 4 mushrooms, chopped
- 1 tbsp olive oil
- 1/2 cup spinach, chopped
- Pepper
- Salt

Directions:

1. Heat 1/2 tablespoon of oil in a pan over medium heat.
2. Add vegetables and sauté for 5 minutes.
3. Heat remaining oil in another pan over medium heat.
4. Add eggs and stir until egg is scrambled and cooked, about 5 minutes. Season with pepper and salt.
5. Add sautéed vegetables in egg and stir well.
6. Serve and enjoy.

Nutritional Value (Amount per Serving):

- Calories 334
- Fat 26 g
- Carbohydrates 6 g
- Sugar 3 g
- Protein 19 g
- Cholesterol 490 mg

Almond Peanut Butter Oatmeal

Preparation Time: 5 minutes

Cooking Time: 5 minutes

Serve: 1

Ingredients:

- 1/2 cup rolled oats
- 1/2 cup unsweetened almond milk
- 1 tbsp peanut butter
- 1 tbsp unsweetened chocolate chips

Directions:

1. Add all ingredients into the glass jar.
2. Cover the jar with a lid and shake well and place it in the refrigerator overnight.
3. Serve and enjoy.

Nutritional Value (Amount per Serving):

- Calories 369
- Fat 20.5 g
- Carbohydrates 35.9 g
- Sugar 1.9 g
- Protein 11.9 g
- Cholesterol 0 mg

Breakfast Kale Muffins

Preparation Time: 10 minutes

Cooking Time: 30 minutes

Serve: 8

Ingredients:

- 6 eggs, lightly beaten
- 1/2 cup unsweetened coconut milk
- 1/4 cup chives, chopped
- 1 cup kale, chopped
- Pepper
- Salt

Directions:

1. Preheat the oven to 350 F/ 180 C.
2. Spray a muffin tray with cooking spray and set aside.
3. Add all ingredients into the mixing bowl and whisk to combine.
4. Pour mixture into the prepared muffin tray and bake for 30 minutes.
5. Serve and enjoy.

Nutritional Value (Amount per Serving):

- Calories 95
- Fat 7 g
- Carbohydrates 2 g
- Sugar 1 g
- Protein 5 g
- Cholesterol 140 mg

Chocolate Overnight Oats

Preparation Time: 5 minutes
Cooking Time: 5 minutes
Serve: 2

Ingredients:

- 1 tbsp unsweetened cocoa powder
- 1 cup rolled oats
- 1 cup unsweetened almond milk
- 1/4 tsp cinnamon
- 2/3 banana
- 2 tbsp walnuts, chopped

Directions:

1. Add banana in a medium bowl and mash using a fork.
2. Add cinnamon and cocoa powder and stir well.
3. Add almond milk and oats and stir to combine.
4. Cover and place in the refrigerator for overnight.
5. Stir oat mixture well. Top with walnuts and serve.

Nutritional Value (Amount per Serving):

- Calories 265
- Fat 9.5 g
- Carbohydrates 40.2 g
- Sugar 5.4 g
- Protein 8.7 g
- Cholesterol 0 mg

Pumpkin Muffins

Preparation Time: 5 minutes
Cooking Time: 2 minutes
Serve: 2

Ingredients:

- 1 egg, lightly beaten
- 2 tbsp pumpkin puree
- 2 tbsp swerve
- 2 tbsp ground flaxseed
- 2 tbsp almond flour
- 1 tsp pumpkin spice
- 1/4 tsp baking powder

Directions:

1. Spray two ramekins with cooking spray and set aside.
2. In a bowl, mix together pumpkin puree and egg.
3. In another bowl, mix almond flour, pumpkin spice, baking powder, swerve, and ground flaxseed.
4. Pour pumpkin and egg mixture into the almond flour mixture and mix well.
5. Pour mixture into the ramekins and microwave for 1-2 minutes.
6. Serve and enjoy.

Nutritional Value (Amount per Serving):

- Calories 131
- Fat 10 g
- Carbohydrates 8.1 g
- Sugar 1 g
- Protein 6 g
- Cholesterol 82 mg

Almond Oatmeal

Preparation Time: 5 minutes
Cooking Time: 10 minutes
Serve: 1

Ingredients:

- 1/2 cup rolled oats
- 1 tbsp almond butter
- 1/2 cup unsweetened almond milk
- 1 tbsp cranberry sauce
- 1/4 tsp cinnamon
- 1/2 cup water

Directions:

1. Add oats, water, and almond milk in a small saucepan and cook over medium-high heat until thickened.
2. Remove from heat and add almond butter and cinnamon and stir well.
3. Top with cranberry sauce and serve.

Nutritional Value (Amount per Serving):

- Calories 278
- Fat 13.4 g
- Carbohydrates 32.8 g
- Sugar 1.4 g
- Protein 9.3 g
- Cholesterol 0 mg

Mushroom Frittata

Preparation Time: 10 minutes

Cooking Time: 30 minutes

Serve: 2

Ingredients:

- 6 eggs, lightly beaten
- 2 oz butter
- 2 oz green onion, chopped
- 3 oz fresh spinach
- 5 oz mushrooms, sliced
- 4 oz feta cheese, crumbled
- Pepper
- Salt

Directions:

1. Preheat the oven to 350 F/ 180 C.
2. Whisk eggs, cheese, pepper, and salt in a bowl.
3. Melt butter in a pan over medium heat.
4. Add mushrooms and green onion to the pan and sauté for 5-10 minutes.
5. Add spinach and sauté for 2 minutes.
6. Pour egg mixture to the pan.
7. Bake in preheated oven for 20 minutes.
8. Serve and enjoy.

Nutritional Value (Amount per Serving):

- Calories 680
- Fat 56.7 g
- Carbohydrates 8.3 g
- Sugar 4.3 g

- Protein 38 g
- Cholesterol 612 mg

Lunch

Cucumber Tuna Salad

Preparation Time: 5 minutes
Cooking Time: 5 minutes
Serve: 6

Ingredients:

- 2 cans tuna, drained
- 2/3 cup light mayonnaise
- 1 cup cucumber, diced
- 1/2 tsp dried dill
- 1 tsp fresh lemon juice
- Pepper
- Salt

Directions:

1. Add all ingredients into the mixing bowl and mix well.
2. Serve and enjoy.

Nutritional Value (Amount per Serving):

- Calories 215
- Fat 13.5 g
- Carbohydrates 6.9 g
- Sugar 2 g
- Protein 16.1 g
- Cholesterol 25 mg

Roasted Parmesan Cauliflower

Preparation Time: 10 minutes

Cooking Time: 30 minutes

Serve: 4

Ingredients:

- 8 cups cauliflower florets
- 1 tsp Italian seasoning, crushed
- 2 tbsp olive oil
- 1/2 cup parmesan cheese, shredded
- 2 tbsp balsamic vinegar
- 1/4 tsp pepper
- 1/4 tsp salt

Directions:

1. Preheat the oven to 450 F/ 232 C.
2. Toss cauliflower, Italian seasoning, oil, pepper, and salt in a bowl.
3. Spread cauliflower on a baking tray and roast for 15-20 minutes.
4. Toss cauliflower with cheese and vinegar.
5. Return to the oven and roast for 5-10 minutes more.
6. Serve and enjoy.

Nutritional Value (Amount per Serving):

- Calories 196
- Fat 13 g
- Carbohydrates 12 g
- Sugar 4 g
- Protein 11 g
- Cholesterol 14 mg

Delicious Chicken Salad

Preparation Time: 10 minutes

Cooking Time: 5 minutes

Serve: 4

Ingredients:

- 1 lb cooked chicken breasts, diced
- 1/2 cup olives, sliced
- 1 tbsp capers
- 2 tbsp olive oil
- 2 tbsp vinegar
- 1/2 cup onion, minced
- 2 tbsp fresh parsley, chopped
- 1 tbsp fresh basil, chopped
- 1/4 tsp chili flakes
- Salt

Directions:

1. Add all ingredients into the mixing bowl and toss well.
2. Serve and enjoy.

Nutritional Value (Amount per Serving):

- Calories 315
- Fat 18 g
- Carbohydrates 3.2 g
- Sugar 1 g
- Protein 33 g
- Cholesterol 100 mg

Cauliflower Mushroom Soup

Preparation Time: 10 minutes

Cooking Time: 26 minutes

Serve: 4

Ingredients:

- 1 1/2 cup mushrooms, diced
- 2 cups cauliflower florets
- 1/2 onion, diced
- 1 tsp onion powder
- 1 2/3 cup coconut milk
- 1/2 tbsp olive oil
- 1/4 tsp pepper
- 1/4 tsp salt

Directions:

1. Add cauliflower, coconut milk, onion powder, pepper, and salt in a saucepan. Bring to boil over medium heat.
2. Turn heat to low and simmer for 8 minutes.
3. Puree the soup using an immersion blender until smooth.
4. Heat oil in another saucepan over high heat.
5. Add onion and mushrooms and sauté for 8 minutes.
6. Add cauliflower mixture to sautéed mushrooms. Stir well and bring to boil.
7. Cover and simmer for 10 minutes.
8. Serve and enjoy.

Nutritional Value (Amount per Serving):

- Calories 260
- Fat 24 g
- Carbohydrates 11 g

- Sugar 5 g
- Protein 4 g
- Cholesterol 0 mg

Creamy Cauliflower Soup

Preparation Time: 10 minutes

Cooking Time: 20 minutes

Serve: 4

Ingredients:

- 1/2 head cauliflower, diced
- 1 small onion, diced
- 1 tbsp olive oil
- 1 garlic clove, minced
- 15 oz vegetable broth
- 1/2 tsp salt

Directions:

1. Heat olive oil in a saucepan over medium heat.
2. Add onion and garlic and sauté for 5 minutes.
3. Add cauliflower and broth. Stir well and bring to boil.
4. Cover and simmer for 15 minutes. Season with salt.
5. Puree the soup using an immersion blender until smooth.
6. Serve and enjoy.

Nutritional Value (Amount per Serving):

- Calories 41
- Fat 1.5 g
- Carbohydrates 4.1 g
- Sugar 2 g
- Protein 3.2 g
- Cholesterol 0 mg

Cauliflower Mash

Preparation Time: 10 minutes

Cooking Time: 10 minutes

Serve: 4

Ingredients:

- 1 lb cauliflower, cut into florets
- 1/2 lemon juice
- 3 oz parmesan cheese, grated
- 4 oz butter
- Pepper
- Salt

Directions:

1. Boil cauliflower florets in the salted water until tender. Drain well.
2. Transfer cauliflower into the blender with remaining ingredients and blend until smooth.
3. Serve and enjoy.

Nutritional Value (Amount per Serving):

- Calories 300
- Fat 27 g
- Carbohydrates 7 g
- Sugar 3 g
- Protein 9 g
- Cholesterol 75 mg

Curried Egg Salad

Preparation Time: 5 minutes
Cooking Time: 5 minutes
Serve: 4

Ingredients:

- 6 hard-boiled eggs, peel and chop
- 1/2 cup light mayonnaise
- 1 tsp curry powder

Directions:

1. Add all ingredients into the mixing bowl and mix well.
2. Serve and enjoy.

Nutritional Value (Amount per Serving):

- Calories 210
- Fat 15 g
- Carbohydrates 7 g
- Sugar 2 g
- Protein 8 g
- Cholesterol 250 mg

Dijon Potato Salad

Preparation Time: 10 minutes
Cooking Time: 20 minutes
Serve: 5

Ingredients:

- 1 lb potatoes
- 1/2 lime juice
- 2 tbsp olive oil
- 2 tbsp fresh dill, chopped
- 2 tbsp chives, minced
- 1/2 tbsp vinegar
- 1 tbsp Dijon mustard
- 1/2 lime zest
- Pepper
- Salt

Directions:

1. Add water in a large pot and bring to boil.
2. Add potatoes in boiling water and cook for 15 minutes or until tender. Drain well and set aside.
3. In a small bowl, whisk together vinegar, mustard, lime zest, lime juice, olive oil, dill, and chives.
4. Peel potatoes and diced and transfer in mixing bowl.
5. Pour vinegar mixture over potatoes and stir to coat.
6. Season with pepper and salt.
7. Serve and enjoy.

Nutritional Value (Amount per Serving):

- Calories 115

- Fat 6 g
- Carbohydrates 15 g
- Sugar 1 g
- Protein 2 g
- Cholesterol 0 mg

Carrot Sweet Potato Soup

Preparation Time: 10 minutes

Cooking Time: 8 minutes

Serve: 4

Ingredients:

- 1 lb sweet potato, peeled and cut into chunks
- 1/2 lb carrots, chopped
- 1 tbsp olive oil
- 1 tbsp ginger, grated
- 6 cups vegetable broth
- Pepper
- Salt

Directions:

1. Heat oil in a saucepan over medium heat.
2. Add carrots and sweet potato and sauté for 10 minutes.
3. Add ginger and cook for 2 minutes.
4. Add broth and stir well. Bring to boil.
5. Turn heat to low and simmer for 20 minutes.
6. Remove pan from heat. Puree the soup using an immersion blender until smooth.
7. Season with pepper and salt.
8. Serve and enjoy.

Nutritional Value (Amount per Serving):

- Calories 218
- Fat 5.8 g
- Carbohydrates 31.4 g
- Sugar 11.2 g
- Protein 10.1 g
- Cholesterol 0 mg

Creamy Salmon Salad

Preparation Time: 10 minutes
Cooking Time: 5 minutes
Serve: 2

Ingredients:

- 6 oz can salmon, drained
- 1 celery stalk, sliced
- 1 avocado, chopped
- 1/2 bell pepper, chopped
- 2 tbsp low-fat yogurt
- 2 tbsp mustard
- 1/4 cup onion, minced

Directions:

1. In a mixing bowl, whisk together yogurt and mustard.
2. Add remaining ingredients and stir to combine.
3. Serve and enjoy.

Nutritional Value (Amount per Serving):

- Calories 405
- Fat 27.8 g
- Carbohydrates 17.5 g
- Sugar 4.6 g
- Protein 24.3 g
- Cholesterol 34 mg

Dinner

Baked Dijon Salmon

Preparation Time: 10 minutes

Cooking Time: 10 minutes

Serve: 6

Ingredients:

- 1 lb salmon
- 3 tbsp olive oil
- 1 tsp ginger, grated
- 2 tbsp Dijon mustard
- 1 tsp pepper
- Salt

Directions:

1. In a small bowl, mix together oil, mustard, ginger, and pepper.
2. Preheat the oven to 400 F/ 200 C.
3. Spray a baking tray with cooking spray and set aside.
4. Place salmon on a baking tray and spread oil mixture over salmon evenly.
5. Bake salmon for 10 minutes.
6. Serve and enjoy.

Nutritional Value (Amount per Serving):

- Calories 165
- Fat 11.9 g
- Carbohydrates 0.7 g
- Sugar 0.1 g
- Protein 15 g
- Cholesterol 33 mg

Dijon Chicken Thighs

Preparation Time: 5 minutes
Cooking Time: 50 minutes
Serve: 4

Ingredients:

- 1 1/2 lbs chicken thighs, skinless and boneless
- 2 tbsp Dijon mustard
- 1/4 cup French mustard
- 2 tsp olive oil

Directions:

1. Preheat the oven to 375 F/ 190 C.
2. In a mixing bowl, mix together olive oil, Dijon mustard, and French mustard.
3. Add chicken to the bowl and mix until chicken is well coated.
4. Arrange chicken in a baking dish and bake for 45-50 minutes.
5. Serve and enjoy.

Nutritional Value (Amount per Serving):

- Calories 348
- Fat 15.2 g
- Carbohydrates 0.4 g
- Sugar 0.1 g
- Protein 49.6 g
- Cholesterol 151 mg

Herb Pork Chops

Preparation Time: 10 minutes

Cooking Time: 1 hour 15 minutes

Serve: 4

Ingredients:

- 4 pork chops, boneless
- 1/2 tsp dried sage
- 1/2 tsp dried parsley
- 2 tsp chives
- 1/2 cup chicken broth
- 1 tbsp butter
- 1 tbsp olive oil
- 1/4 tsp pepper
- 1/4 tsp salt

Directions:

1. Preheat the oven to 350 F/ 180 C.
2. Spray a baking dish with cooking spray and set aside.
3. Season pork chops with pepper and salt and place in prepared dish.
4. In a small bowl, mix together butter, oil, sage, parsley, and chives.
5. Rub butter mixture on top of each pork chops.
6. Add broth in the baking dish around the pork chops.
7. Cover with foil and bake for 1 hour.
8. Remove cover and bake for 15 minutes more.
9. Serve and enjoy.

Nutritional Value (Amount per Serving):

- Calories 317
- Fat 26.4 g

- Carbohydrates 0.3 g
- Sugar 0.1 g
- Protein 18.7 g
- Cholesterol 76 mg

Taco Chicken

Preparation Time: 5 minutes

Cooking Time: 6 hours

Serve: 4

Ingredients:

- 1 lb chicken breasts, skinless and boneless
- 2 tbsp taco seasoning
- 1 cup chicken broth

Directions:

1. Place chicken in the slow cooker.
2. Mix together chicken broth and taco seasoning and pour over chicken.
3. Cover and cook on low for 6 hours.
4. Shred chicken using a fork.
5. Serve and enjoy.

Nutritional Value (Amount per Serving):

- Calories 233
- Fat 8.7 g
- Carbohydrates 1.7 g
- Sugar 0.5 g
- Protein 34 g
- Cholesterol 101 mg

Broiled Fish Fillet

Preparation Time: 5 minutes

Cooking Time: 10 minutes

Serve: 2

Ingredients:

- 2 cod fish fillets
- 1/8 tsp curry powder
- 2 tsp butter
- 1/4 tsp paprika
- 1/8 tsp pepper
- 1/8 tsp salt

Directions:

1. Preheat the broiler.
2. Spray broiler pan with cooking spray and set aside.
3. In a small bowl, mix together paprika, curry powder, pepper, and salt.
4. Coat fish fillet with paprika mixture and place on broiler pan.
5. Broil fish for 10-12 minutes.
6. Top with butter and serve.

Nutritional Value (Amount per Serving):

- Calories 224
- Fat 5.4 g
- Carbohydrates 0.3 g
- Sugar 0 g
- Protein 41.2 g
- Cholesterol 109 mg

Yummy Chicken Bites

Preparation Time: 5 minutes
Cooking Time: 10 minutes
Serve: 2

Ingredients:

- 1 lb chicken breasts, skinless, boneless and cut into cubes
- 2 tbsp fresh lemon juice
- 1 tbsp fresh oregano, chopped
- 2 tbsp olive oil
- 1/8 tsp cayenne pepper
- Pepper
- Salt

Directions:

1. Place chicken in a bowl.
2. Add reaming ingredients over chicken and mix well.
3. Place chicken in the refrigerator for 1 hour.
4. Heat grill over medium heat.
5. Spray grill with cooking spray.
6. Thread marinated chicken onto skewers.
7. Arrange skewers on grill and grill until chicken is cooked.
8. Serve and enjoy.

Nutritional Value (Amount per Serving):

- Calories 560
- Fat 31 g
- Carbohydrates 1.8 g
- Sugar 0.4 g
- Protein 66 g
- Cholesterol 200 mg

Grilled Chicken Breasts

Preparation Time: 10 minutes

Cooking Time: 15 minutes

Serve: 4

Ingredients:

- 2 lbs chicken breasts, halves
- 6 tbsp fresh parsley, minced
- 6 tbsp olive oil
- 1 1/2 tsp dried oregano
- 1 tsp paprika
- 1 tbsp garlic, minced
- 6 tbsp fresh lemon juice
- Pepper
- Salt

Directions:

1. Pierce chicken breasts using a fork. Season with pepper and salt.
2. Add lemon juice, oregano, paprika, garlic, parsley, and olive oil into the zip-lock bag.
3. Add chicken to the zip-lock bag.
4. Seal bag and shake well and place in the refrigerator for 1-2 hours.
5. Heat grill over medium-high heat.
6. Place marinated chicken on the grill and cook for 5-6 minutes on each side.
7. Serve and enjoy.

Nutritional Value (Amount per Serving):

- Calories 625
- Fat 38 g
- Carbohydrates 2 g

- Sugar 0.6 g
- Protein 65 g
- Cholesterol 200 mg

Chili Garlic Salmon

Preparation Time: 5 minutes
Cooking Time: 2 minutes
Serve: 3

Ingredients:

- 1 lb salmon fillet, cut into three pieces
- 1 tsp red chili powder
- 1 garlic clove, minced
- 1 tsp ground cumin
- Pepper
- Salt

Directions:

1. Pour 1 1/2 cups water into the instant pot and place trivet into the pot.
2. In a small bowl, mix together chili powder, garlic, cumin, pepper, and salt.
3. Rub salmon pieces with spice mixture and place on top of the trivet.
4. Seal the instant pot with a lid and cook on steam mode for 2 minutes.
5. Once done, release pressure using the quick-release method than open the lid.
6. Serve and enjoy.

Nutritional Value (Amount per Serving):

- Calories 205
- Fat 9 g
- Carbohydrates 1.1 g
- Sugar 0.1 g
- Protein 30 g
- Cholesterol 65 mg

Baked Lemon Tilapia

Preparation Time: 10 minutes
Cooking Time: 12 minutes
Serve: 4

Ingredients:

- 4 tilapia fillets
- 2 tbsp fresh lemon juice
- 1 tsp garlic, minced
- 1/4 cup olive oil
- 2 tbsp fresh parsley, chopped
- 1 lemon zest
- Pepper
- Salt

Directions:

1. Preheat the oven to 425 F/ 220 C.
2. Spray a baking dish with cooking spray and set aside.
3. In a small bowl, whisk together olive oil, lemon zest, lemon juice, and garlic.
4. Season fish fillets with pepper and salt and place in the baking dish.
5. Pour olive oil mixture over fish fillets.
6. Bake fish fillets in the oven for 10-12 minutes.
7. Garnish with parsley and serve.

Nutritional Value (Amount per Serving):

- Calories 252
- Fat 14.7 g
- Carbohydrates 0.5 g
- Sugar 0.2 g
- Protein 32.2 g
- Cholesterol 85 mg

Garlic Shrimp

Preparation Time: 10 minutes

Cooking Time: 50 minutes

Serve: 8

Ingredients:

- 2 lbs large shrimp, peeled and deveined
- 1 tbsp parsley, minced
- 1/4 tsp chili flakes, crushed
- 1 tsp paprika
- 6 garlic cloves, sliced
- 3/4 cup olive oil
- 1/4 tsp pepper
- 1 tsp kosher salt

Directions:

1. Add all ingredients except shrimp and parsley into the crock-pot and stir well.
2. Cover and cook on high for 30 minutes.
3. Add shrimp and stir well.
4. Cover and cook on high for 20 minutes.
5. Garnish with parsley and serve.

Nutritional Value (Amount per Serving):

- Calories 258
- Fat 18.9 g
- Carbohydrates 3 g
- Sugar 0.1 g
- Protein 21.5 g
- Cholesterol 162 mg

Chapter 6: Snacks & Desserts

Chocolate Avocado Pudding

Preparation Time: 10 minutes

Cooking Time: 10 minutes

Serve: 6

Ingredients:

- 2 avocados, chopped
- ¼ cup creamy almond butter
- 1 tsp vanilla
- 1 tbsp unsweetened cocoa powder
- 1 cup semi-sweet chocolate chips
- 1 cup unsweetened almond milk

Directions:

1. Add chocolate chips and almond milk in a microwave-safe bowl and microwave for 30 seconds. Stir well and microwave for 30 seconds more or until chocolate is melted.
2. Add vanilla and cocoa powder and stir well.
3. Pour chocolate mixture into the blender. Add remaining ingredients and blend until smooth.
4. Pour pudding into the serving bowls and place in the refrigerator for 30 minutes.
5. Serve and enjoy.

Nutritional Value (Amount per Serving):

- Calories 248
- Fat 13.4 g
- Carbohydrates 28.7 g
- Sugar 21.5 g

- Protein 3.5 g
- Cholesterol 0 mg

Frozen Berry Yogurt

Preparation Time: 5 minutes

Cooking Time: 5 minutes

Serve: 6

Ingredients:

- 4 cups frozen blackberries
- 1 tsp vanilla
- 1 tbsp fresh lemon juice
- 1 cup full-fat yogurt

Directions:

1. Add all ingredients into the blender and blend until smooth.
2. Pour blended mixture into the container. Cover and place in the refrigerator for 2 hours.
3. Serve and enjoy.

Nutritional Value (Amount per Serving):

- Calories 60
- Fat 0.9 g
- Carbohydrates 11.6 g
- Sugar 7 g
- Protein 1.8 g
- Cholesterol 0 mg

Raspberry Sorbet

Preparation Time: 5 minutes

Cooking Time: 5 minutes

Serve: 4

Ingredients:

- 12 oz frozen raspberries
- 1 tbsp honey
- ¼ cup of coconut water

Directions:

1. Add all ingredients into the blender and blend until smooth.
2. Pour blended mixture into the container. Cover and place in the freezer for 2-3 hours.
3. Serve and enjoy.

Nutritional Value (Amount per Serving):

- Calories 61
- Fat 0.1 g
- Carbohydrates 15.5 g
- Sugar 13.3 g
- Protein 0.4 g
- Cholesterol 0 mg

Mixed Berry Popsicles

Preparation Time: 5 minutes

Cooking Time: 5 minutes

Serve: 10

Ingredients:

- 1 cup fresh blackberries
- 1 cup fresh blueberries
- 1 cup fresh raspberries
- 2 tbsp fresh lemon juice
- 2 cups strawberries, sliced
- 2 tbsp honey

Directions:

1. Add all ingredients into the blender and blend until smooth.
2. Pour blended mixture into the Popsicle molds and place in the freezer for 4 hours or until set.
3. Serve and enjoy.

Nutritional Value (Amount per Serving):

- Calories 44
- Fat 0.3 g
- Carbohydrates 10.7 g
- Sugar 7.6 g
- Protein 0.7 g
- Cholesterol 0 mg

Strawberry Yogurt

Preparation Time: 5 minutes

Cooking Time: 5 minutes

Serve: 6

Ingredients:

- 1 lb frozen strawberries
- 1 cup non-fat yogurt
- 1 tsp liquid stevia

Directions:

1. Add all ingredients into the blender and blend until smooth.
2. Pour blended mixture into the container.
3. Cover and place in the refrigerator for 2-3 hours.
4. Serve and enjoy.

Nutritional Value (Amount per Serving):

- Calories 87
- Fat 0 g
- Carbohydrates 19.8 g
- Sugar 12 g
- Protein 1.8 g
- Cholesterol 2 mg

Chia Seed Pudding

Preparation Time: 5 minutes

Cooking Time: 5 minutes

Serve: 4

Ingredients:

- ½ cup chia seeds
- 1 tsp liquid stevia
- 1 ½ tsp pumpkin pie spice
- ½ cup pumpkin puree
- ¾ cup unsweetened coconut milk
- ¾ cup full-fat coconut milk

Directions:

1. Add all ingredients into the mixing bowl and whisk well to combine.
2. Pour into the serving bowls and place them in the refrigerator for 2 hours.
3. Serve and enjoy.

Nutritional Value (Amount per Serving):

- Calories 275
- Fat 24.5 g
- Carbohydrates 9.9 g
- Sugar 3.3 g
- Protein 5.3 g
- Cholesterol 0 mg

Avocado Hummus

Preparation Time: 10 minutes

Cooking Time: 5 minutes

Serve: 4

Ingredients:

- ½ avocado, chopped
- 2 tbsp olive oil
- ½ tsp onion powder
- 1 tsp tahini
- ½ tsp garlic, minced
- 1 tbsp lemon juice
- 1 cup frozen edamame, thawed
- Pepper
- Salt

Directions:

1. Add all ingredients into the blender and blend until smooth.
2. Serve with vegetables.

Nutritional Value (Amount per Serving):

- Calories 215
- Fat 17 g
- Carbohydrates 10 g
- Sugar 0.3 g
- Protein 9.1 g
- Cholesterol 0 mg

Chocó Protein Balls

Preparation Time: 5 minutes
Cooking Time: 10 minutes
Serve: 15

Ingredients:

- 1 tbsp unsweetened cocoa powder
- 1 tsp vanilla
- 3 tbsp pistachios, chopped
- 1/3 cup chia seeds
- 1 cup almond butter
- 1 ½ cup oats

Directions:

1. Line baking tray with parchment paper and set aside.
2. Add all ingredients into the mixing bowl and mix until well combined.
3. Make small balls from mixture and place on a prepared tray and place it in the refrigerator for overnight.
4. Serve and enjoy.

Nutritional Value (Amount per Serving):

- Calories 55
- Fat 2.4 g
- Carbohydrates 6.7 g
- Sugar 0.2 g
- Protein 2.1 g
- Cholesterol 0 mg

Conclusion

The book contains simple and comprehensive information about gastric sleeve bariatric surgery and post-surgery diet plans along with healthy and delicious recipes allowed after gastric sleeve surgery. These recipes are divided into four different stages of diet after surgery. In this book, I have discovered many delicious recipes easy to make and tasty